Methods Of Persuasion: How To Turn A No Into A Yes

I0422154

By George Lucas

Table of Contents

Introduction

Do you ever wish for the power or ability to control and lead other people to accepting your line of thinking? The ability to speak to people and convince them to do a thing helps someone to win complex negotiations or ward off a tough opponent. The simple techniques are widely used even in relationships when you have to get the attention of someone and make her give in to your moves.

Methods of Persuasion: How to turn a No into a Yes is a great book that will assist you to overcome the fear that is related to speaking your mind out, get attention from your audience and make the desired impact. It is all about psychology where you need to master your oratory strengths and know how to unlock the defensive strategies of the audience. You need to understand the defensive secrets in the human behavior.

Methods of Persuasion: How to turn a no into a yes is a sizeable book that offers you various techniques that lead to winning the hearts of the people you meet and speak to, and the techniques include rapport, body language, neuro linguistic programming and assertiveness.

Many people have used these techniques including professional negotiators, neuro linguists and other specialists. The strategies used are mainly benevolent but you are not limited to using unethical means, if at all they are only supposed to make your audiences comply to your persuasion, but the motive should not be oppressive at all.

The techniques discussed in this book have been researched for long and most of them have been in used since the evolution of the human kind. It is the nature of man to strive to survive and from a long time, he has been using the ability to convince other to tow the line and give in to his thinking.

Powerful persuasive techniques are used in the business world too in these modern times, where a company sends its representatives to potential customers physically or online to make them buy their services and in the process increase the sales. The companies use subtle techniques to neutralize resistance from customers and lure them to buying their services.

Similar techniques are required in sociology too where in order to induce attraction in romantic situations some secret methods of persuasion have to come into play to enhance emotional manipulation. These techniques come naturally to many people in the natural setup of the progression of life.

You will need to learn these secrets so that you can incorporate them into the normal human relations, offer you self-confidence, mental strength and the will to step up and approach those who you want to persuade.

Chapter 1: The Major Approach

Most people find it hard to make their friends or partners react to what they want, but it is never a complicated affair when you have all the required techniques at your fingertips. Methods of Persuasion offers you those techniques and extra advice to enable you overcome the barrier of expressing yourself and drawing attention to you, thus making people do what you want. The power to persuade people is entrenched in you and all you need is to understand specific things such as the power on non-verbal communication. Here you need to know how to use facial expressions, the tone of your voice and specific gestures to draw attention and stress a point thus conquering a situation.

Body language is another thing that you need to work on, which is a two-way process. Your body language can have a great impact on how your audience will react to your moves, and their body language will tell you how your approach is working on the person's mind too. At times, you ought to be cunning and relay signals that will make your talk charming and relaxing, and by so doing, the audiences will easily give in to your persuasion.

Remember a bold person always takes control of a given situation. Your approach hence needs to show courage so that your audiences can have trust in what you are telling them. Courage is achieved when you understand your rights and know how to apply them without feeling guilty of what you are doing. It even becomes enjoyable when you pour your thoughts and see the effect of appreciation on people's faces. Assertiveness enables you to overcome problematic situations, and when you get through them, you can use your success to make people understand the importance of the things you are telling them.

Understanding the mind of your audience is another thing that you should practice, because you will be able to influence their thinking to benefit your objectives. It becomes very enjoyable to know that you are saying the things that will sway a person's thinking to accepting what you say, because when you sharpen this technique no one will object what you say to them.

As you embark on reading this book, understand that you will face a lot of resistance that is meant to derail your progress. It comes from lack of willingness to listen and general negativity that hinders communication. The book offers techniques to handle emotions and present your case without much of resistance. Read through and let the book transform your life with the simplicity of swaying other people to your way of thinking.

Immediate Impact

Hesitation is never tolerated when it comes to persuasion because you will not appear to have the confidence that is required. You should hence try to make immediate impact when you set to make someone buy your idea. You can achieve the impact by using the power of your body language. You can convey strong emotions simply by the way you present yourself. Your body language should show authority and openness. You should however be very careful not to show a hint of anxiety, resistance or untrustworthy, because that will push your audience away.

You should allow your prospect to do a first sight judgment and take you as likeable, friendly and competent in doing the persuasion.

As you carry on with your initial approach, expect resistance for the first time from your prospect, and since it cannot be portrayed to you verbally, body language on the prospect's side will be a great tool to detect it. Detecting resistance from the audience's is easy because they will show conspicuous behaviors like giving you a sided look, leaning away from you, crossed legs and arms, minimized eye contact, uneasy gestures like tapping fingers or foot and basically trying to face away from you. When your prospect reacts with these kinds of body posture and language, try to adopt a more positive reaction to counter the negative attitude shown towards you through the body language. Bring ease into the approach by modifying the tact to make whatever you are saying a bit appealing, even if it is not sinking well into the mind of the prospect.

~ Body Language - You can tell if your Idea is Being Appreciated

Your prospect's body language speaks volumes and you can easily tell if your idea is being appreciated or not. Appreciation will be shown through an open posture, which indicates acceptance. The reaction is psychological and even the prospects never realizes that he or she is striking such a pose. They will always maintain eye contact, feet pointing towards you and the stroking of the chin.

Make yourself open in such a situation to bring out a relaxed mode of conversation and in that case, you will be able to engage the person into a deep conversation that will lead to persuasion. When you both have the positive posture, the final result will not be less than an agreement.

Body Language that tells you there is Cooperation

When a prospect is in the verge of buying your idea, eye contact will be maintained for more than 70%, not to mention that it will be followed by a genuine smile. The prospect will lean towards you and try to shorten the distance between the two of you. He will always nod to let you know that he is following your talk to the letter. The legs will be uncrossed and arms open, probably placed on the table.

Expect Suspicion

A closed posture will tell you that your ideas and talk is not fully appreciated. The prospect will appear uneasy with the hands deep into the pockets. There will be no eye contact and the little that there will be the prospect might be looking at you from the corner of his eye. That definitely tells you that he is not ready to agree to your idea. You need to pull up your socks in this situation because such prospects are very hard to convince.

Counter this pose with a positive one so that your audience can feel a bit at ease, and maybe give it bit by bit. Avoid showing any of suspicion by working hard in improving your body language. By doing so, you will be able to make the prospect feel at ease and eventually give you the attention you need to drive your point home.

Always remember that the prospects will mostly be looking for a sign of lies in your approach and talk, and hence you have to be bold and maintain eye contact at all times. Your hands should be free and relaxed, because when you cover your mouth frequently, tug your ears or rub your nose more than usual, it will make you look fishy and it will derail your effort.

Always keep in mind that liar is always uncomfortable and will keep on shifting in the seat or shuffling the feet throughout the conversation. Keep yourself comfortable in the room and be completely at ease, not as if you are ready to dash out of the room at any minute. The prospect will not take that lightly and will detect a sense of lies in you, not to give you his whole attention and eventually you will not succeed in persuading them.

Body language is powerful when communicating and it comes naturally to express the influence of the talk. We may be unaware of the meaning of the language but the message is passed perfectly when we see the gestures and movements of the body that are elicited by the conversation at hand. It will make you feel insufficient in your effort to convince someone when their body language shows that they are not comfortable with the situation. You should hence derive a way to work around the resistance ad ease the situation because if you carry on with the conversation, it will have to flop eventually.

Learning the body language is not as complex as studying the alphabet because for starters it is an inborn thing and you only need to perfect the way you see the behavior of your audience. Understand the combination of postures that show discomfort, mistrust, suspicion and other negative reactions that are brought about by a conversation. In countering them, learn the postures that will make the prospect see that your persuasion is harmless and you are not trying to mislead him or her.

Chapter 2: The Main Skills of Persuasion

As you continue reading Methods of Persuasion: How to turn a no into a yes", you will understand that the ability to convince people to do a thing that is from your mindset is not a natural God-given gift, as many people perceive it to be. You can practice it and eventually be among the people who can speak their mind and make others follow their ideas. Remember that you need to be positive in everything you do, although that is taken care of in this book, where you will be guided of the moves to make, the way to handle your prospects and pass the message in a way that it will remain genuine.

Listeners can take in a positive message but get varying understanding, and so you should follow the given guidelines in this book to make sure that your approach remains steadfast so that your message can be understood positively.

The following are the major skills of persuasion that you should equip yourself with whenever you want to sway people towards your thinking or make them accept your advances. Remember practice makes perfect and so you should have these skills ready so that you do not struggle when communicating to people. It should not appear as if it is a script you have mastered to use whenever you are persuading people, because if you are too uniform and monotonous you will not last long in this profession of persuasion.

~ Boldness

Being courageous of what you are doing offers you a sense of authority, and when it comes to persuasion, you will have an upper hand in handling the situation. You are the boss of your ego and hence have the rights to control your actions, which should however be in line with positive expectations of human conduct. A person who wants to have the ability to persuade others should be dignified to put himself at a respectable pedestal.

Respect is earned and you should earn yours by recognizing the rights of your prospect, otherwise you your boldness will appear negative as if you are trying to be a controller and not a guide.

Boldness enriches the confidence in you where you get the energy to push on even if when you encounter resistance. Never show weakness on your face when you are under pressure from a difficult prospect because you will meet many such characters in the process of conversation. The way you portray yourself tells people how they should treat you. Politeness is part of being assertive because that is when you get the chance to be reasonable in your persuasion. Avoid a situation where the prospect will struggle to understand your motive. Be open with whatever you are saying so that you can guide your listener to understanding your aim.

It is natural that one cannot succeed in persuading others without having an assertive character. It has to be entrenched in you so that you can convince others to do something because a weak person will never conquer the minds of people who are ready to correct you in a bid to keep your advances at bay.

A victorious persuasion is not hard if you can understand your rights first and take your stand in the conversation. The next thing should be to arrange the persuasion tools you need to deploy such as making the audience feel that you are in control of the situation. Some things you do in the initial stages of the persuasion determine the grip and control you will have, for instance invoking the right mental setup of the person you are speaking to, and that depends on the level of assertiveness that you apply.

You may wonder how one can be assertive and that is normal because some people think that assertiveness requires that you be aggressive, which is a wrong perception. You need to balance passiveness and aggression so that you can defend your rights in polite way, and still show your listener that you are in control of what you are saying.

Do not allow apprehension to take control of you because this is a major problem with many people, who fear to speak out their minds when they get into a situation of persuading others. Be dominant but not oppressive because exaggerated dominance will make mild-mannered listeners to coil away from fear, while your aim is to attract them and make them listen to you.

Your activities should be in line with people's civil liberties, which mean that you ought not to violate them. The rights are indicated below so that you can etch them on your memory.

- Everyone has the liberty to state what he or she wants
- Expression of opinion
- Make own decisions
- Withhold opinion or fail to give an explanation regarding the persuasion
- Decline a request that comes from the communication
- Comply to a request but with conditions

When working on persuading someone you should be guided by the following steps, which will help you to leave no doubt on the mind of your prospect.

- **Be Forthright** – Avoiding beating around the bush when you need to drive a point home. Put your thoughts, ideas and needs into words and do not fear about the outcome if at all you are doing it right. The advantage of it is that you will not have any excuses of your approach.

- **Be Accountable** – Opinions are personal and hence you should let the audience understand that whatever you are telling them is not a global theory but how you think that things should be done. People will be more attentive to you when you open up and perceive you as having a strong will. Statements such as "My understanding is....", "My feeling is that....", "I think that..." and "In my opinion..." should depict accountability.

- **Be Calm and Composed** – Your body language, tone of the voice and words should work in moderation to make the listener feel your self-control.

- **Be Polite** – You can hurt someone feelings without knowing when you use inappropriate words. You should hence avoid any character or personal attacks in your conversation.

~ **Defend your moves**

You will meet people with complex personalities who will try to hinder you from taking control of your actions. You will need the following persuasion techniques that will help you to avoid such characters and be able to take tough situations head on.

Inducing Acceptance for your Request

You may have requested something form someone but the request was turned down, which is always a frustrating experience when you know that your request was genuine and called for, but you got a regret result instead. Persistence is a technique that you can apply to get the right response that you need, although the waiting time could be a bit longer. Actually many people apply it unconsciously.

It is an easy process where you simply need to set the outcome that you would want for that request, and then keep on repeating the request that is supposed to elicit the response that you need.

This technique requires that you practice a lot of composure, politeness and determination. Your tone should always be friendly regardless of the times that you are going to repeat the process. The respondent may become agitated because of the monotony of your request and hence it could be prudent to rephrase the statement. The unwavering repetition will in the process weaken the resistance to your request.

Dealing with Criticism

We hate criticism but we cannot avoid it. It weakens us and most of the times hurt us so badly, and the bad thing is that we experience it at least once per day. Most people deal with it emotionally, which is a bit risky because when handled wrongly it can escalate to uncontrollable heights where relationships might be wrecked.

The solution to this threat is to use clouding technique and handle criticism assertively. This technique removes all the venom that is elicited by criticism, and people can converse at an understandable level where they easily come into an agreement. Clouding the criticism means that it's potential to cause verbal war is neutralized, which is done by accepting the situation, taking in the claims and ignoring the effects that it was meant to cause. Listening and speaking about it instead of fighting to deny the claim achieves positive solutions easily.

We have five steps of clouding the criticism and they are discussed below.

- Start with dissecting the content of the criticism and not the behavior of the vessel, who is the critic. Never be emotional when listening to the content because it will result to more criticism when it weakens you and leaves you more vulnerable. Just as blood lures sharks, fury leads to more criticism.

- Do not stop the opponent until he or she exhaust all that they want to say about you, and do not interrupt. Keep silent all the way. He has the chance to pour all the fury and at the same time, you will be in a better position to counter his sentiments. After listening to him, you will have a clear-cut rebuttal that will be enough to neutralize the criticism. An emotionally drained critic is an easy target for a perfect counter-attack.

- Before you answer, ask the critics if they have anything left that they would like to add, so that you can ensure all the embers are eliminated.

- Inform them that you already have the wind about it with a statement such as "I know you are worried about...", and this thwarts the danger of the critic getting into everyone's mind with the information.

- Cloud the criticism by partially agreeing with the things that have been said, which is a perfect way to ensure that you clean all the trails that the critics may use with follow up attacks. Do not be aggressive with the accusations and instead accept the truth in them. The friendly approach will always give you an upper hand when dealing with it.

When clouding criticism and partially accepting the sentiments, the attacker is left with no arsenal because a critic is always ready for a fight the accusations. The partial agreement makes the attacker to cool down and in that case, you both can settle down for an open and controlled discussion. For instance, you might be accused of always being away on weekends to an extent that you do not visit your friends regularly, and you might answer affirmatively adding that you are working on a project that is taking most of your free time. You therefore agreed about the accusations partially, but offer a concrete explanation after that.

You can also cloud the criticism by agreeing to its principle but not the main accusations. While the principle might be valid, you ought to object the blame. The critic will be confused by the manner you have agreed without putting up a fight, and before he regains the balance, you will be on the next step of putting out the remaining members of the accusations.

After you cloud the criticism, do not leave it at that. Ask the critics to offer ideas that would make the situation better. Give them your ear and at the end speak you mind on what you think the best solution should be, but always try to water down all the negativities that the criticism could have caused. Presume innocence and settle the case in a way that it will appear like it was erroneous. This will save the critic's faced and rub off the effects of the criticism.

This technique works wonders by cooling things down and allowing the power of rapport to take center stage. When you presume innocence of the critic, he or she will have the space to save face when you engage him in a positive session of questioning. You therefore create the ground of interrogating the person at a reasonable level guided by facts. You may question how the criticism relates to your normal lives, and even find that you were on the wrong and save face too. The best outcome is that your non-threatening interrogation will make the critic come back to his senses and enable him to correct himself in a bid to avoid another similar situation.

Create Demarcations When you say No

When you answer allegations to the affirmative and a negative answer was expected, you destabilize the plans of your attacker and make him lose self-esteem. However, there are times when you need to stand your ground and say no without giving excuses. The 'no' should be expressed with calmness in the tone of your voice and how you handle your body language. Practice saying no when simple situations arise so that when you are met with a major accusation you can use the technique to ward off the accusers.

In situations where you do not need to agree or refuse, for instance when you can agree in part, a firm yes works properly where you then agree to what the accuser is saying but with clear demarcations of what you like and do not like. For instance, when you are needed to work longer, you can agree but set a limit of the extended time.

You are supposed to set demarcations in situations such as when your generosity is taken for granted to an extent of being wasted.

~ **React Positively**

Maintaining an assertive personality is not very hard but you have to sweat it out before you mould it to the level that it can be termed as perfect. They say practice makes perfect and that exactly applies here. You may have stayed behind the scenes for so long in your life but through practice, you can be assertive and maintain it in a natural way. All you need to do is replace the weak areas in your character with a strong character and work on it to make it stick.

As you read Methods of Persuasion, you will learn the tricks of changing that character through the change of vocabulary, getting rid of some sentences and switching to a new way of speaking. You will need to learn how to resolve specific issues in a definite manner. The following exercises will help you to be assertive in all situations even subconsciously.

Exercises that will build your Behavior to become Persuasive and Influential

- Replace "should" with "will" because the former shows a weaker personality than the latter. When you say, "I will....." you show decisiveness and the expectation of people you are speaking to will be for the positive results of what you are to do. It builds an inner confidence that tells you that you are the ultimate judge of your actions, thus making you to work harder towards your goal.

- The word "can't" is a no no, always answer to the affirmative when you are asked whether you can accomplish a task. When you feel that you can accomplish it, explain how you can do a similar thing that will bring even better results. Your attitude changes to the better when you avoid the "I can't" phrase, and you will always get the courage to tackle any task that is thrown at you. Giving alternatives shows that you can go to any lengths to offer solutions.

- Tailor your questions in such a way that the respondent cannot answer with a simple YES or NO. The respondent should be put in a position where he can only answer with an explanation. For instance, a question such as "Can I assist you?' can be answer with a simple yes or no but another such as "How can I assist you?" will require an answer that will elicit a conversation. The latter style of questioning shows that you really want to assist and makes the respondent to engage you in a talk.

- The word "but" never exists in an assertive and persuasive personality and hence you should avoid it like plague. Let it be replaced by the word "and" whenever it needs to be used. The reason to avoid this word is that it negates the positive news that comes before it. For instance, when one says "We accomplished the task, but..." tells the listener that the positive of accomplishing the task were spoiled by some occurrence after that. When you switch "but" with "and", the message will sound more optimistic.

- Switch fear with power to give your mind the strength to deal with quaky situations. This mostly happens in relationship set up where you meet a person of the opposite sex and the mind goes blank. It is a natural feeling but the problem about it is that gives you the fear of failure. You should not be thinking about how you may fail to succeed. To fight this feeling you should stop thinking about you and think of the person before you, and fixate your mind to expect a positive result from the engagement. Shift your thinking to what the person may be thinking at that moment and put yourself in her shoes. You will eventually start thinking of the words to use and entangle her from the fear of meeting you.

- Be like a tiger, it never believes that it can fail regardless of the outside forces. When you have such a strong mental capacity, you are not prone to fear and so failure will not be an option in the process of persuading people.

- Take control of your voice and use a slow, balanced and even tone. Do not rush your words because you will eventually find yourself raising the pitch of your voice. When it gets high you will be perceived to be anxious and without authority. When you want to persuade someone, always remember to reduce your speaking speed to 40%, and speak with pauses that have a downward pitch. The firm pauses give you that authority to stay in control of the conversation while the person listening follows word by word.

- Your speech should go hand in hand with your gestures, and do not exaggerate the gestures. Move your arms and facial expression in harmony and with precision.

- The perceived personal space is your territory and you should guard it completely. The authority you have in the conversation shows the amount of space that you command. You can therefore increase it if you want by being more assertive, but in the process remember that your partner may also want to put boundaries and deny you the extra space. One way to create space is to ensure your side of the table if seated has your briefcase or belongings placed comfortably, or simply using your gestures comfortably without irritating other with vigorous movements.

- Another strong tool when you want to be more persuasive and assertive is the eye contact. A strong gaze that is unwavering will weaken a strong opposition. Note that it might be a bit tricky to win the eye contact war if you are dealing with an aggressive person. They use the eyes to weaken their opposition and hence you ought to be ready and stand your ground. Counter the gaze with unwavering stare and look directly at the middle of the person's eyes, and thus you will give them an illusion that you are reading their minds. Practice this technique and you will find out that it will. simplify your effort of persuading people particularly the ones who cannot maintain eye contact for long.

- Warding off an unpleasant character who cannot stop talking can be done easily by the use of his name. There are people who will not give you the chance to speak, because they do it nonstop and what you are left with are short acknowledgments of the topic, even though you might be bored to the bone. In that case, you can cut that person off by calling his by his name, and then immediately take over with a summary of what he was saying. Make it sound like the conversation has ended as you summarize the talk. However, be polite and indicate that you can carry on with the discussion at a later date.

~ Understand what Fuels You

Yu ought to understand the things that motivate you to want to persuade others to do certain thing. You have to know what is in store for you, or what you will achieve when you persuade a person successfully. The concept works just like in the case of an employee who works hard for the monthly payment, and the caregiver who focuses on the progress of patients to ensure that they recover and eventually feels great after they are well. Another example is a manager who ensures all is well for the smooth running of a company to maintain his position and prosper, and similarly you should strive for something that would come after the persuasion, so that you can have the will to push on.

The people you enter into a dialogue with have an ultimate reason for engaging you in the dialogue, and when you understand what they need you will have an upper hand over them. Do not try to block their objective of dialoging with you, and instead hold a dialogue that makes them see that they have a lot to gain when they comply with what you are telling them. Hide your needs in what the person wants from the talk and in that case, you will have your way and win the debate very easily.

Because you definitely want the person to agree with you, you will have to weigh the benefits you offer to find out if they can serve his needs, because only then he can agree to your persuasion, and you will have won clean and square.

In our normal human lives, we have ten main requirements or needs that need to be satisfied in the things we do on a daily basis. You should hence try to understand those needs of the person you want to persuade, and identify the ones that are pressing him the most at that particular time. When you note it, you can then carry on with phrasing your request in a way that he will have no other option but to agree to your request, and in the process satisfy the need.

Note the following general requirements that you can identify to favor you in the time of persuading a person.

Self-esteem – Is the passion to be recognized and appreciated

Superiority – The need to progress and achieve a lot

Safety – The need to be secure physically, socially, financially and in any other factor of life

Affection – The need to be loved

Greediness – The need to have it all

Power – The need to be the main guy

Acknowledgement – The need to have individual worth

Pride – The need to showoff

Freedom – The need of controlling every aspect of your life

Privacy – The need to secure your space

Of all the above-mentioned needs, self-esteem takes the center stage because and lack of it may make someone lose the meaning of diligence. Everyone wants to have a strong feeling of self-worth and hence you can use that to persuade people to yield up to your request. As long as you can make a person feel special because of accepting your request know that your advances will be accepted with open arms.

Use praise to get to the heart of your target. Self-esteem is usually boosted when a person receives praises of any kind, as long as they are in line with the subject at hand. This can be seen in a working environment where employees always feel motivated by praises from their bosses, and in return, they work hard to achieve more of what is making their bosses happy.

In persuasion, ensure that you direct your praises to the area that when the target yields to your praises, he will try to prove to you that you are right and in return give into your request so that you can confirm that you are right about his character. People require recognition to lift their self-esteem and that can be a great tool to make a person accept your request.

Use reputation to make a person yield to your request. Instead of going directly to your requirement and forcing the person, you listen and act on what you want. Try to show him how he has kept a good name by doing the good things to people in previous situation, and then tell him how you would like a similar favor from him. That person will definitely want to keep the good name by yielding to your request. However, it is always good to add that you do not require the favor because he had done it to other but because it is important to you in a certain way. An example is where a person may want a pay raise, and after persuading the employer through his reputation, he adds that he would like an increment to cover the vacuum that is left by the increasing bills.

It is natural to be easy and relax around people who need us. This is a requirement that helps people to stay together and help each other, and it is a strong tool that you can use to lure your audience and make them comply with your persuasion. When you make a person feel that you need him, he will know that his contribution is very important to you and hence will not pull back or reject your request. However, do not misuse the tool like politicians do. You should have reasonable demands that the person can offer.

Acknowledge someone's superiority and you will be amazed at how they comply with your persuasion. Create a scenario where you are out of ideas and the knowhow to do something, and make the person that you want to persuade understand that you know he can get you out of the hook with his great ideas. Request a bit of his time to resolve what you need and seize the opportunity to engage him in a persuasive conversation. You have the guarantee that no matter how you approach the subject, that person will be more than ready to listen to you because how you caught his attention created a picture in his mind that he is the only solution to your problem.

Men behave in specific ways to accomplish things that sustain their main needs, and when you understand the various vital needs that makes a man stand tall and want to be among the best, and then you can use the ability and show them how you can help them achieve the needs. In the process, you will be working on how to use their help in making them yield to your persuasion. The advantage of this trick of persuasion is that the person will never feel that you have taken advantage of him, which you have not really taken, but will look at it from the perspective of benefitting from your compliments and making him feel worthy and proud.

~ Use Rapport

Rapport has a magical link to persuasion. This technique is a balanced way of using words to pass a message in a manner that everyone will want to listen to you. Unlike the previous styles of persuasion that we have read about, this one is a bit physical and does not involve tricking the minds of your listeners. You have to learn how to arrange your words so that you can influence others. You can however combine the technique with the previous ones whereby you understand or learn the minds of your listeners, and then tailor your words to manipulate their thinking to your advantage.

Rapport assists you to create a harmonious attachment when you handle yourself at the same level as your listener. As a result, the prospect will be more comfortable and trustful. A comfortable environment emanates bringing the two of you together through attraction, and at such a time, persuasion becomes very simple.

To get a clear picture of how this works, try to remember any of the conversation you ever held with another person before, and why it always reflects on your mind. The things that made that special moment be etched on your mind are the power of rapport. The attachment of such a conversation is always powerful to an extent that you can tell the next words that are to come from the mouth of your partner. It becomes a balanced communication where both of you are patient and very attentive when one is speaking.

Rapport grows where there is a liking between the two of you, but that does not means physical attraction. The balanced exchange of words and information brings about the attraction. When both of you are drowning deep in to the conversation makes it appear like a dream.

The best thing about this tool is that it can be feigned when you want to persuade someone. When done professionally, it will generate a situation just like the one in a genuine situation. You need to make your listener feel the attachment so that he can surrender and engage you in the conversation that will lead to your requests. The first step is to make the person like you or feel like you have the same ideologies. In that case, you need to gather information about that person or simply ask him some questions prior to the dialogue, and you will have an idea of what the person is like.

You will also need to make the person feel some similarity between the two of you, because it is human nature to feel safe around people who we share similarities. It makes the mind relaxed in a manner that you can persuade him with simplicity. As long as you can make the person like you then you will have won the battle of persuasion halfway.

You can generate rapport in various ways to make the person be attracted to your style, but you do not have to pick any style of generating it because you can combine all of them to create a stronger approach to persuasion.

You may have experience a situation where a friend of yours tends to change is tone and accent just to be at the same wavelength of the person he is speaking to. This mostly comes naturally when you want to bring yourself at the same wavelength and ease the tension that may be generated by your varying accents and tones. When you want to simplify the situation, you can then try to copy the personality of the person you are speaking to, so that you can both be at a neutral conversing level. The fun about this tool is that you can be like many people in different situations when you want to persuade them.

Copy every aspect of the person's behavior even the moods just to make him feel the attachment. When he feels down, feign the mood and state that you feel bad because if his situation. What you should always avoid is to make him feel worse by belittling his feeling. This is for example giving him hope that the situation is just for a short time and things will be good soon. Such a statement will spoil the attachment and make it look like his being down is his own making and hence he should hold on for the moment. The trick is to show him that all he is doing is normal and you support him in the bid to correct the situation.

You will be in a good position to start a conversation that will lead him to follow your advice when you make it look like you are sharing the same problem. He will take it easy after you show him that you both are alike and your problems are safe with each other, and hence trust will build between the two of you. This is a perfect technique that will make compliance thrive because the mind of that person you want to persuade will feel that it is all safe to mingle with a source of solution, which is you.

The process of making the person feel at ease, safe and okay should go on for a few minutes and then you can start advancing towards your goal of persuading him. This is after you bond perfectly so that you can be assured of an eventual agreement. The set up should be to give the person some suggestions of solutions to the situation, he is already psychologically manipulated to think that you are the ultimate solution for his state and hence he will easily give in to your suggestions.

Avoid jumping into conclusion that the person is ready for persuasion if you are not sure that you have achieved your goal. You can simply do this non-verbally by checking various physical responses such as facial expression and the body posture. The rate of speech and tone of his voice will tell you how comfortable he is with your suggestions or approach. You can test him by mirroring his posture and gestures to see if his will blend with yours after a short time, and if he does then you know that you are on the safe side because rapport has been created and you can then execute your objective of persuasion.

What happens if the person does not give in to your approach and rapport? This always happens and you need to understand that you do not always have your way in every approach. The person may react negatively and hence you will need to have a lion's heart in dealing with the situation. Do not give up but try to make the person feel supported through a different approach. The main objective should be to make his situation bearable so that he can listen to you. As you engage him in a conversation, he will feel as if he is having a mono dialogue with himself. According to him, you are a part of his situation and thus will be free to speak in order to improve the situation.

Rapport has huge rewards and you should practice it to achieve your goals in different situations. If at all you can be able to establish and maintain a link with the person you want to persuade, then you can put the technique to use in different scenario such as personal relationships, business deals, legal situations and other areas that require negotiations to reach a certain objective.

~ Be Persuasive Verbally

The verbal technique is a great to persuasion. It is the technique that salespersons use in order to thrive in their trade, and you can perfect the same too if you want to b a great persuader. The technique requires a precise arrangement of phrases and words that are guided towards a definite objective. The point where the rapport left the job of persuasion is where the technique of verbal persuasion takes over. It is used to make your motives clear on the minds of your listeners and hence make them do or believe something.

You need to be keen on how you arrange your words, phrases and paragraphs in a balanced sequence that will keep the listener glued to you not to lose a word so that he can understand your conversation. Spice your talk with examples that you can take from the surroundings, keeping in mind that the success of your effort will at times depend on the situation and surroundings. You ought to deploy the technique with care to achieve maximum success.

One of the best ways to achieve positive results in persuasion is to presuppose that what you want to do has already been done, or the person has already agreed to your requests and the result is positive. In that case, you are supposed to phrase your talk in a past tense form, in a manner that denotes that your listener has already agreed to your proposal. To keep yourself going you will need to tell your mind that your listener is enjoying your talk, a technique that will make you try harder to please your listener and make him yield to your request.

This technique works perfectly when you want to strike business deals where you want to create an excellent image in the minds of the entrepreneurs you are speaking to.

As a normal human being, we always feel the need to appreciate the good that has been done to us, and the urge to return the favor becomes like a debt that we feel we should pay. The feeling generates to a kind of a mental burden that we need to relieve. In a bid to relieve the mind off the burden, a person will feel the need to do a thing that will be bigger than the favor he was given.

The reciprocity reflex action is normal to everyone and you can simply note it with a simple polite action like a smile. When a person smiles at you even if it is a stranger, it is very hard that you will refuse to smile back. A good compliment is responded to in a kind way too, and they are all powers of trying to reciprocate and repay the god feeling that is brought about by the good deed.

The same aspect is used by bigger organization when they want to generate funds, they can fundraise by calling people to a luncheon where the people will be told of the idea that is making the organization needs the funds. In return, to the nice cuisine that the people get, they will want to appreciate and offer or pledge the amount they have for the good course. The amazing thing is that most people will want to give more than the value of the food and refreshments they have enjoyed.

When a company is in need of stepping up its performance, the executive does not go directly to the employees to tell them how they are supposed to up their game. It will definitely not go down well with many employees, and in most cases, they will rebel if there is no incentive to the change of operations. The executive of the company can achieve the same objective, if they arrange a retreat to a different environment for a number of days, maybe over the weekend. At that time, they can allow the employees to enjoy themselves at the expense of the company, and in the process give them the idea of the changes in order to improve the performance of the company. The amazing results could be that the employees will embrace the suggestion in unison, given that their effort would be rewarded with pay increment incentive.

You can use the same concept when you want to lure or persuade a person. A small favor or gift would be enough to set grounds for a good negotiation. Gifts are always offered in public or openly and hence, they cannot amount to be called bribes. The rate of gift rejection is also very low and hence the there must be the urge to reciprocate the goodies that you offer to people. In that case, when you plan to request something after offering a gift, the chances are that the person will give in to your requests.

If the gift concept does not work well for you, then you can use another mostly used technique that is a bit psychological and confuses the mind of the targeted person to make him feel that he ends up as the winner. The technique involves of coming up with two similar request, the first one being a major one that you are sure that the person you want to persuade will not agree to. Then there is the second request is what that you exactly want the person to give in to. You approach the person with the first request and chances are that he will say that it is not possible. You will then immediately ask for the lesser request, which is exactly what you want and bingo! You will have achieved your objective through that very simple technique.

Another technique is where you elicit commitment of your prospect by asking a series of requests that are easy to give in to, and after you ask a series of them, say for instance three requests that the person will agree to, then you can introduce the major request that you are interested in. Given that the person has already given in to the previous requests, it will be very difficult for him to reject the fourth one, not realizing that it is the min request that you are interested in. The mind of that person is deceived to believe that it will not be a good picture to reject that final request after giving in to the previous ones, and you will have won the duel again! The idea is to ensure that all the requests you ask are related and are easy to accept with the important one coming last.

Before you start your requests however, it is prudent to entice the person with a low cost if you want make a special sale. The terms may be changed as the transaction nears the when the buyer cannot pull out of the deal. The explanation of the price change has to be realistic in order to keep the confident that the buyer has in you intact.

We still have another technique that is referred to as Pace and Lead. The technique entails asking a series of requests or questions in your conversation. The pace requests should elicit affirmative answers and they should be a number of requests to camouflage the lead request, which is your main catch. Since the person you are persuading will be taking the requests positively as they have to be genuine, the main one that you are seriously interested in will sail through without a struggle.

You can use attribution to persuade a person do something. A person who is orderly for example will always be doing things that are in line with orderliness and cleanliness, such as picking dropped trash or arranging things in a room. In persuasion, you can create the same positive behavior in a person, when you want him to be doing what you perceive as right always, and the person will believe that he can be so, and start practicing the positive things you are telling him.

You can start by creating a scenario where things are not working right and give a desired solution, with an example of a person that practices the solution to achieve positive results. You can then persuade a person by letting him understand that to be positive you simply ought to do that simple action on a daily basis and the situation will change to positive and remain so as long as the person maintains the good deed.

Chapter 3: Advanced Skills of Persuasion

The main techniques we have talked about earlier can suffice to convince and persuade a person in a normal general setting, but there comes a time when you have to handle a difficult person. Stubborn people can make it hard for even the most experienced persuaders, but with the skills that you will read here in Methods of Persuasion: How to turn a no into a yes, you will not have any trouble handling such a person. You need to equip yourself with excellent skills that will enable you to deal with another professional persuader because you never know whom you are to encounter in life.

The trick is the knowhow to arrange words and other verbal tools that will make a person ease the opposition and accept to your requests.

Dealing with Objection

Difficult person are hard to persuade because they are always ready to object and show you how something cannot work. The best way to deal with such objections is to water it down immediately indicating that your theory has been use in other places and worked. Doing so will help you to stop further escalation of the objection. You can let the person know that you understand his worries and it should not be a problem because your other clients have gone the same route and succeeded. Examples are very important in this situation, and assure the person that he will not be alone in it because you will guide him through it.

Some objections are not real and are only meant to distract your progress. From the many objections you receive, check the genuine ones and deal with them, you can ignore the others and still succeed.

Reverse psychology is a tool that will also help you to achieve your objective, where you can let the prospect know that it is his responsibility to carry on with the proposal, and you might withdraw it if he delays any further. The trick makes him generate the fear of losing should he fail to take your proposal

~ **Secrets of Breaking the Ice**

This applies to persuasion based on intimacy. Most men generate a lot of fear when they want to get the attention of a beautiful lady, and hence they are engulfed in a plethora of questions that play in their minds over and over when wondering how they can persuade a lady to like them. In a natural human setting, a lady will never make the first move but will show you interest if she also like you. Do not stay on the sidelines because you will lose a golden chance given that attractive ladies are a clear target for any potential man. So, make the first move!

For you to start a relationship you need to get a reaction and it does not come before you act. Clear the fear in your mind by powering it with positive and optimistic thoughts of how the relation will be once the lady agrees to your request. Positive thoughts will make you relaxed and hence adrenaline will not rush when you approach the person. Adrenaline can mess your chance of winning the heart of the lady. They have a way of choosing the right man by looking for particular traits in those who approach them, and when you start shaking, clamming your hands, mumbling inaudible words or gestures that show you are not confident they will give you time to explain yourself but will not take you moves seriously.

~ **Easing the Emotions**

Every man gets nervous in such situations, the solution is to breathe deeply and slowly for a few seconds to lower the heart rate, and when you feel okay, you can then approach your target.

Practice the best opening lines that will not scare her away and as you continue you can throw in some compliments or simple questions. Before you compliment you will need to study her well to notice genuine traits that you like so that you can talk about them. False compliments will spoil your effort. Allow her time to talk when she shows signs of chipping into the conversation. Some ladies will want to ask a lot about you and you should be genuine or if you do not feel like answering to all the questions you can give her a different one that answers her indirectly.

When you take the first shot at initiating a relationship, you ought to understand that it works with the same concept as farming. You need to prepare the farm and plant seeds, water and fertilize them and then you can harvest. It has challenges but when you work hard, you will get the best harvest. Love on the other hand requires you to initiate the first move and expect challenges such as rejection, but you need to hold your head up high and show that you can take anything that comes your way until you get the acceptance of your life partner.

Chapter 4: Go for the Jugular

The art of persuasion is not for the fainthearted because you have to be prepared to meet all kinds of challenges, some of which are very disheartening. That notwithstanding, there are people who do the persuasion perfectly and achieve magnificent results, but you need to understand that there is no special education that they attend to get where they are. It is all about practice, perseverance, enjoyment, and learning the human behavior. When you understand the behavior and know their weak and strong points, you can apply the right techniques to tackle the weak points and make them do as you wish.

Confidence plays a great role when it comes to persuasion and you can attest that by looking around the successful individuals around you. They have the courage to face their business partners, customers and any other person that they would want a favor from, or make them strike a business deal. The amazing thing is that people will get attracted to persuasive and courageous people as they look upon them with envy. Self-confidence will take you a long way in your quest for the mastery of persuasion.

Believe in yourself and master your intelligence and skills, and do not forget that humility will help you interact with people because they feel accepted when communicating with you. When you draw people towards you through your humility, you got to have the ability to express yourself and guide their minds towards your idea. Effective persuasion is the ability to transfer information from your brain to their brains, which should be accepted by them as their own. For it to be accepted you will need to show them the benefits of that information that you offer them.

The ability to make them accept it will need a clear understanding of the motivation that drives your audience, whether a single person or a group. The motivation is what you will use to drive your points home when you touch on it directly. Your requests should be realistic so that you can be able to counter objections.

Structure your communication in a clear way that will be possible for the audience to follow you step by step. The audience should be aware of where your talk is leading so that they can make decisions in their minds whether to accept your requests or not. Ensure that the subject is on your fingertips because when questions come from the audience you will not want to start stammering or appearing lost. Be bold and master the subject, not just a compilation of data that you will have with you, but also an in-depth knowledge of all the issues that entail that subject. This is because you need to have a firm ground when responding to the challenges that the audience will throw at you, more so when the audience is ready to disagree with your motive.

You will learn the persuasion skills very easily when you practice the following steps.

The nagging approach will work for you at the most unexpected situations. You may have encountered a person who talks too much when addressing people, and the talk may sound nagging but will eventually work for him, when the audience give in to his requests just to make him end the talk. The audiences exchange the compliance with peace that will come from the end of the nagging talk.

When you do not have to be nagging, you can use an alternative of making your request urgent, and then hope to make those who you are requesting see that compliance is required within a short period. Uniqueness will help you attract the attention of your audience, and in the process of their excitement, you pass your message. Make your request useful too. Many people will want to participate in an activity if it is enjoyable or has to offer something in return.

If you want to persuade people then you should show them the importance of why they should follow your directives. Useful persuasion gives you an upper hand in the negotiations because the audiences will consider why they need to use their precious time on your ideas, if it sound feasible then majority will want to try it. Make your request specific so that people do not have to struggle when executing your request. If it is about selling a product, let them know how to use it or the time it takes for a service to be delivered on request. The process should also be user friendly. You can offer guarantees like refunding money if the request does not work, while you very well know that whatever you are telling the is doable and will deliver the expected results.

Proof it beyond reasonable doubt that after they follow your directives there will be rewards maybe in form of profits or measurable statistic. Realistic testimonials will help you proof everything.

~ The Art of Seduction

Everyone strives to put food on the table, have some good clothing and shelter too. Even though we can get those basic things in abundance depending on how hard we strive, we will always need love. Love however does not come naturally because it has to natured between two strangers through seduction. If you achieve that, the happiness will follow you as your life follows the right direction.

People thrive on love because you can have everything in this world but without love, you will enjoy none. Love is linked to psychology and to stabilize it you will need to offer love and receive it in the same measure. Handling it in the right way is the main concern to many, because if mishandled it can break clans or ruin a nation. Peace is found where love thrives.

All good things generate from love and hence the power of it can never be taken easily. As oxygen is vital to human life, so is love, which gives life.

Love is all about psychological principles where you ought to express it through special actions and words that will fulfill the emotional needs of the special person you want to start a relationship with, and they also need to respond in equal measure. You however need to work hard to attract them to you, so that you can express your feelings and motive.

The first step of seduction should be to initiate attraction that will be followed by liking and hence you will get the ball rolling. The next thing that comes after initiating attraction will be contact where the two people express their feelings physically.

There is a misconception that the first move should always be made by the male partner, but things do not have to be so, because women too can engage a man but in a lighthearted engagement.

Practice to listen because it is one way to win the battle of love, and you will also get to learn some things about the targeted partner. However, listening is not enough and you therefore need to show similarities between the two of you.

Psychology shows us that we get attracted and like those who have similar traits like ourselves.

If you have to praise her do it in realistic way. Do no flatter her during the first meeting because it might drift to the wrong direction. Not genuine things about her like an attractive tattoo on her shoulder, her cute bag or her composed walking style. Do not praise her too much though, it might work negatively for you, and if you do it less than expected she might wonder what type of a man you are if you cannot note the nice things in a woman. Little praise also makes her wonder how she can please you if you cannot note anything about her.

Be easy in everything you do, it is the initial part of the relationship and hence you ought to balance things and make the partner comfortable in the life before you.

~ Attractive Voice and Sweet Tongue

Away from seduction, we look at how the power of your voice affects your ability to persuade. The biggest percentage of our communication depends on our voices. A balanced speech helps us to convey ideas and express our needs. It is prudent therefore to check if your voice works for or against your bid to persuade.

Your vocal quality has the same importance just as the content you are offering to your listeners. A good sign that you are not doing good in your speech making is when the listener keeps interrupting you to ask you to "say that again". The factors that affect your voice are tempo, timbre, speed, inflection and resonance among others. If you can balance these factors then you are on a good course to deliver your message perfectly and clear. You should be worried when one of them goes off balance, for instance when you are too fast and the listener cannot keep up with the speed. It is hence vital to ensure that your voice is at its best before you present a speech that you want the listener to follow and act in a certain way.

The confidence in your voice should be felt throughout your talk. If your voice gets weak it will make your persuasive character dull and you will not realize your goal, which can be ordering, wooing or persuading. Next, we will look at how you can enhance your voice to give it the energy and confidence it requires to make you a perfect persuader.

Stomach Energy – Inexperienced speakers power their voices from the chest but that is not the way to do it, because the voice will not have the energy to make it full and authoritative. One cannot be able to maintain constant sentences without releasing the breath from the stomach. Practice this technique by applying pressure on your stomach and speak at the same time. The act of exhaling from your stomach will help you voice your words at the same time. That fullness of your voice is what is required throughout your speech, but when you depend on the shallow air from your chest, you will never achieve the authority that strong voice offers to a speaker.

Hype your words to make the speech catchy, by applying emotional bouts of words that will entice the listeners as well as make them alert. You do not want to speak to an audience that is dozing off or staring on their mobile devices, they can be disheartening to you too.

Your posture is another factor that affects your speech delivery. Even when you are speaking to a single person, he can judge your confidence from your posture. You slouch and your words will not be audible and you will even look weak. No one will trust persuasion from a weak speaker. Be confident and stand tall, and make use of your area by moving around or making some simple gestures that go along with your conversation.

Use descriptions effectively to try to make clear images in the mind of your listener, of what you are speaking about. Professional persuaders can describe a situation and make it seem real just like you were there when it was happening. The same technique can make the person you are persuading see the action you want them to do in virtual reality.

In the summary of how you should your voice, you need to keep in mind that the things you say are vital, but the way to say them is even more important. In that case, use the power of your voice properly.

~ Strive to be the Best

Many people who want to be the best in this field practice the art of persuasion to ensure that they remain the best. The more you practice is the more you will get the hook of it and be among the best. There are masters of persuasion that you will meet out there and hence you ought to be ready to be put to test through objections and counter attacks.

After reading Methods of Persuasion: How to turn a No into a yes however, you will have nothing to fear because all that you need is explained in this book, and so what you are left to do is enough practice of persuading people to accept your requests without feeling as if they are being taken advantage of.

Learning never ends and hence you will have to check more techniques of persuasion to improve your persuasion ability. No one is born with the skills of moving masses with the power of words, or persuading people to do certain things willingly, but you can be the best when you learn these great skills of not only persuading but also connecting with the ones you are speaking to.

Conclusion

Learning these skills can take a bit of time but remember patience pays. Take time to develop persuasion skills and you will have power to lure people to do lovely things. The power you will get is because people will be trusting what you say. After you get set with those skills, you are good to enjoy your success in influencing and persuading others in every kind of setting, which can be the work place, at home or your friends.